AMAZING
STRUCTURES

Amazing Ancient Structures

CAROLINE THOMAS

REDBACK
publishing

Redback Publishing
PO Box 357 Frenchs Forest NSW 2086
Australia

www.redbackpublishing.com.au
orders@redbackpublishing.com.au

ISBN 978-1-925860-92-4

Author: Caroline Thomas
Designer: Redback Publishing

Originated by Redback Publishing
Printed and bound in Malaysia

Acknowledgements
Abbreviations: l—left, r—right, b—bottom, t—top, c—centre, m—middle
We would like to thank the following for permission to reproduce
photographs: (Images © shutterstock), p3b, WH_Pics , p4tr, p24-25 Drone
Explorer, p5cr, p22bl Amazing Travels, p8bl denisbin (CC BY-ND 2.0), p9tr,
p30bcr Public domain, via Wikimedia Commons, p12bl tristan tan, p17tl
leoks,
p17tcl p17tcr, p17tr Alexey Fedorenko, p17bl NASA, Public domain,
via Wikimedia Commons, p21tr Gary Todd, CCO, via Wikimedia Commons,
p22r, p31tr dadao

Every effort has been made to contact copyright holders of any material
reproduced in this book. Any omissions will be rectified in subsequent
printings if notice is given to the publisher.

Contents

ANCIENT

North
America

Central
America

South
America

U.K.
2
1

Ancient Landmarks Key

1 Carnac Stones, France

2 Stonehenge, England

3 The Colosseum, Italy

4 The Parthenon, Greece

5 The Pyramids of Giza, Egypt

6 Petra, Jordan

7 Persepolis, Iran

8 Terracotta Warriors, China

9 The Great Wall of China

10 Brewarrina Fish Traps, Australia

All over the world, ancient civilisations built structures, buildings and whole cities that continue to amaze us today. People travel far and wide to marvel at their beauty and endurance, and to learn about the people who built them.

LANDMARKS

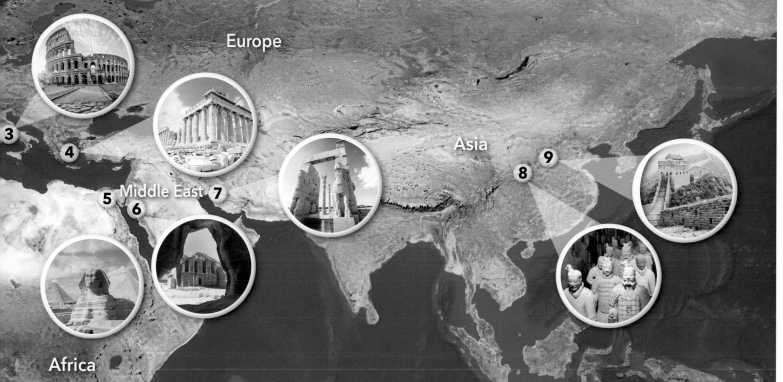

Europe

Asia

Middle East

3

4

5

6

7

8   9

Africa

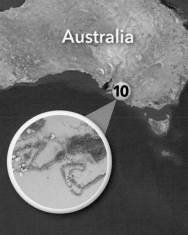

Australia

10

Historic Achievements

The manpower and tenacity it took to create these structures, in eras when there were no construction cranes or bulldozers, is inspiring. Many of these structures were the vision of one person but were often erected using slave labour. Artisans and craftsmen carved intricate images into solid rock, which now provides us with information about these ancient cities and peoples.

ABORIGINAL ENGINEERS

Australia's ancient structures are some of the most ancient in the world and are of incredible historical value. Long before civilisations in Egypt or Rome were building their impressive structures, Australian Aboriginal people were building theirs.

Historic Homes

On Rosemary Island, located in the Dampier Archipelago off Western Australia, **archaeologists** have uncovered some of the earliest known domestic structures in Australia.
They date between 8,000 and 9,000 years old, which means they were built around the end of the last Ice Age. The structures are circular foundations that would have once been homes with multiple living spaces. One area was used for grinding seeds while another held the remains of shells gathered for food. People also most likely slept and lived in separate areas.

The Original Rock Stars

The Archipelago of 42 islands and the nearby Burrup Peninsula in Western Australia are known as, Murujuga, in the language of the Ngarluma people. The Burrup Peninsula contains more than one million rock engravings and is one of the densest concentrations of petroglyphs in the world. Some of the art is over 30,000 years old.

BREWARRINA FISH TRAPS

The oldest man-made structure in the world is in Australia, in the small town of Brewarrina, New South Wales. The Brewarrina Fish Traps form an ancient structure that is ten times older than Stonehenge. Known to the local Ngemba people as Baiame's Ngunnhu, the fish traps are possibly the oldest known human-made structure on earth, dating back as far as 40,000 years old.

Trapped eels were harvested into baskets

Budj Bim Eel Traps

For over 6,600 years, the Gunditjmara people lived in a permanent village and maintained a successful eel industry. This is recognised as being unique in the world's human history of settlement and society, as it disproves the belief that Aboriginal people were only nomadic hunter-gatherers.

The landscape in the area was created by the eruption of Budj Bim (Mount Eccles) around 27,000 years ago. The Gunditjmara people used this site to engineer and construct an extensive aquaculture system with weirs and dams that included traps for eels. This region is also a traditional meeting place and ceremonial site for the Gunditjmara people.

George Augustus Robinson

Hidden Ingenuity

The first European to note the eel traps was Chief Protector of Aborigines, George Augustus Robinson. In 1841, he recorded finding –
'… *an immense piece of ground, trenched and banked, resembling the work of civilised man but which on inspection I found to be the work of the Aboriginal natives, purposefully constructed for catching eels.*'

The eel traps were approximately two kilometres in length and covered a huge area about the size of 11 modern football fields. The systems included hundreds of metres of excavated and natural lava channels and dozens of basalt block dam walls.

Early European settlers ignored any evidence of Aboriginal engineering or irrigation. It was an inconvenient truth that the land they were claiming was already settled and occupied. In the 1970s, a team from the Victoria Archaeological Survey re-discovered the extensive Aboriginal fish-trapping system.

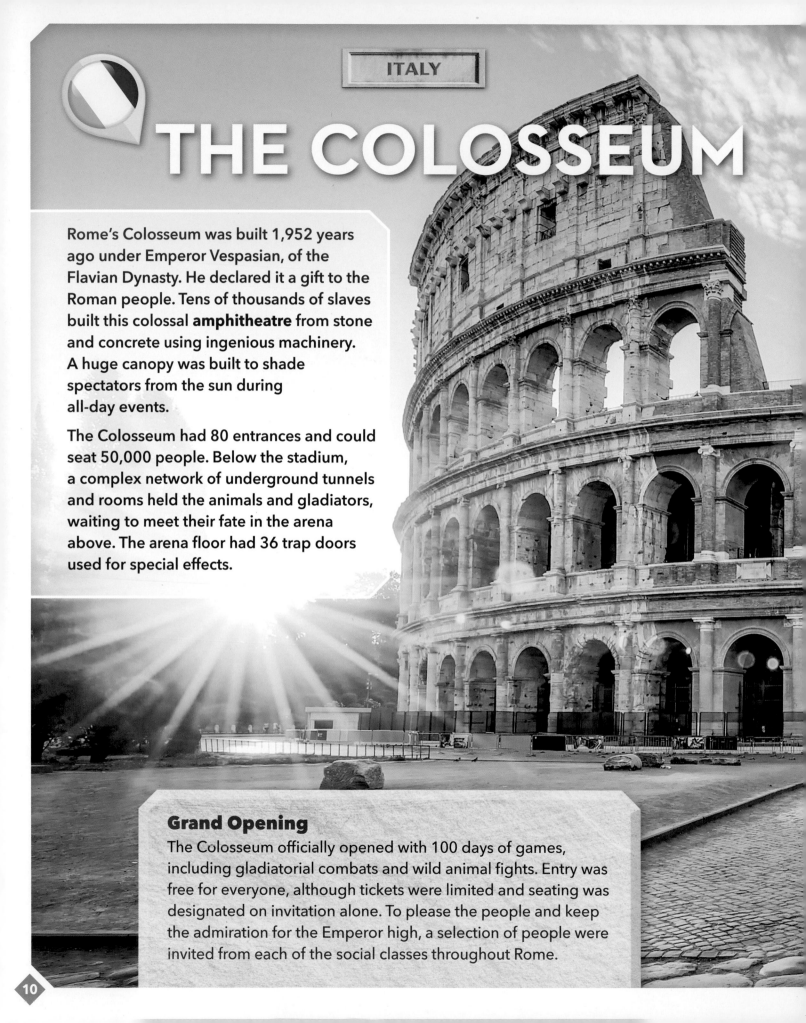

THE COLOSSEUM

Rome's Colosseum was built 1,952 years ago under Emperor Vespasian, of the Flavian Dynasty. He declared it a gift to the Roman people. Tens of thousands of slaves built this colossal **amphitheatre** from stone and concrete using ingenious machinery. A huge canopy was built to shade spectators from the sun during all-day events.

The Colosseum had 80 entrances and could seat 50,000 people. Below the stadium, a complex network of underground tunnels and rooms held the animals and gladiators, waiting to meet their fate in the arena above. The arena floor had 36 trap doors used for special effects.

Grand Opening

The Colosseum officially opened with 100 days of games, including gladiatorial combats and wild animal fights. Entry was free for everyone, although tickets were limited and seating was designated on invitation alone. To please the people and keep the admiration for the Emperor high, a selection of people were invited from each of the social classes throughout Rome.

Deadly Entertainment

The Colosseum is known for its gladiators. They were usually former slaves that were trained to fight to the death. They fought for the entertainment of others and shows often included wild animals and various props including weaponry. Some shows involved teams of gladiators, where teams of trained slaves were forced to fight teams of paid professionals.

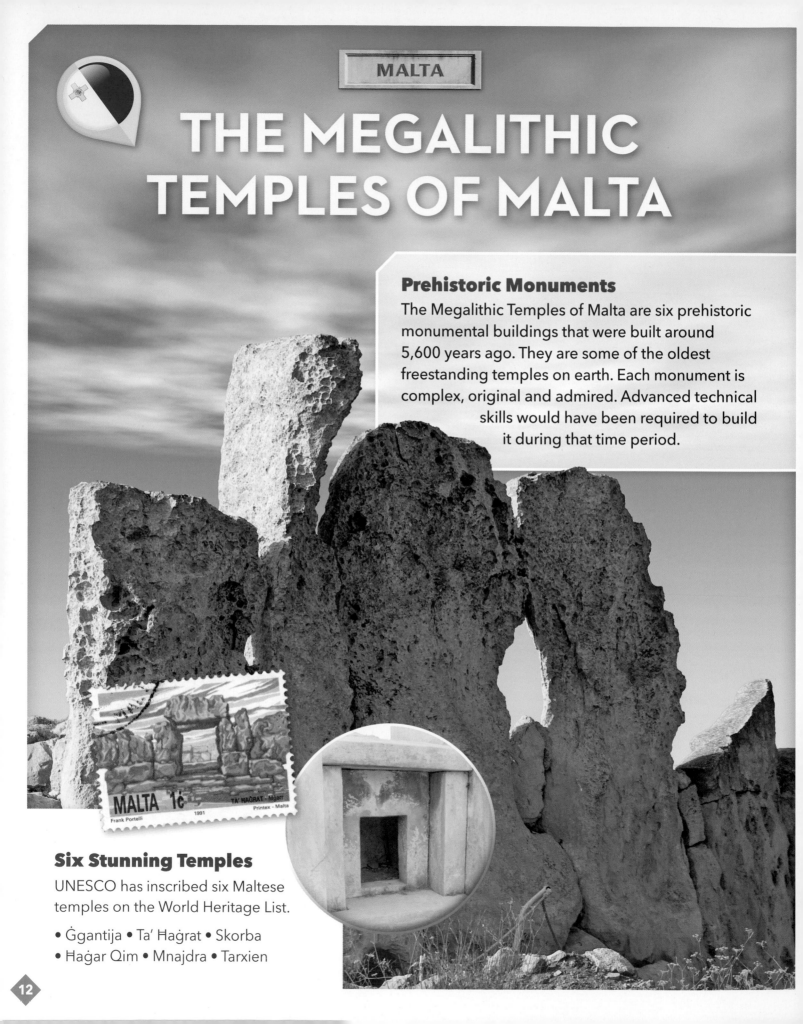

THE MEGALITHIC TEMPLES OF MALTA

Prehistoric Monuments

The Megalithic Temples of Malta are six prehistoric monumental buildings that were built around 5,600 years ago. They are some of the oldest freestanding temples on earth. Each monument is complex, original and admired. Advanced technical skills would have been required to build it during that time period.

MALTA 1c TA' ĦAĠRAT · MĠARR
Frank Portelli 1991 Printex - Malta

Six Stunning Temples

UNESCO has inscribed six Maltese temples on the World Heritage List.

- Ġgantija • Ta' Ħaġrat • Skorba
- Ħaġar Qim • Mnajdra • Tarxien

PERSEPOLIS

An Ancient Capital

Persepolis was an ancient capital of the Achaemenid Empire, the second Iranian dynasty. It is an impressive palace complex, built on an immense half-artificial, half-natural terrace. The largest building in Persepolis is the Apadana Hall which includes 72 carved columns. Persepolis was designated a UNESCO World Heritage Site in 1979.

The Gate of All Nations

Visitors to Persepolis who wished to visit the Royal Palace were made to pass through the Gate of Xerxes, otherwise known as The Gate of All Nations. The gate led to an audience hall where they were sorted into social importance before being guided through one of three doors that led to different parts of the palace.

GÖBEKLI TEPE

The World's First Temple

Predating Stonehenge by 6,000 years, Göbekli Tepe is considered to be the world's first temple, having being built about 11,000 years ago. This megalith was crafted and arranged by people who had not yet developed metal tools. Göbekli Tepe is formed with at least 20 circular installations that contain several pillars surrounded by walls. There are about 200 pillars throughout the whole temple. The tallest pillars tower five-and-a-half metres high and can weigh up to ten thousand kilograms.

Cult of the Dead

Göbekli Tepe appears to be a central location for a cult of the dead. The site is also home to rock statues with carvings of animals that appear to protect the dead, dating back as far as 12,000 years. In 2018, the site was designated a UNESCO World Heritage site.

CARNAC STONES

The Carnac stones are the largest collection of megalithic standing stones in the world. These 3,000 prehistoric standing stones are of local rock and were erected by the pre-Celtic people of Brittany. The actual purpose of the rocks remains unknown although some people believe they were used to track the movement of the sun or the stars.

THE PYRAMIDS

The **pyramids** of Egypt are incredible structures. They were built during a time when Egypt was one of the most powerful civilisations on Earth and Egyptian pharaohs were viewed as being somewhere between human and divine. Pyramids were royal tombs that were built with stepped sides to help the pharaoh climb to heaven and join the gods.

Pyramids of Giza

The most famous pyramids in Egypt are the Pyramids of Giza, near the capital of Cairo. They were constructed around 4,500 years ago. The three main pyramids in Giza are the Great Pyramid of Khufu, the Pyramid of Khafre and the Pyramid of Menkaure. Each pyramid is part of a larger complex that includes buildings such as a palace, temples, boat pits and smaller pyramids that entomb other royal family members.

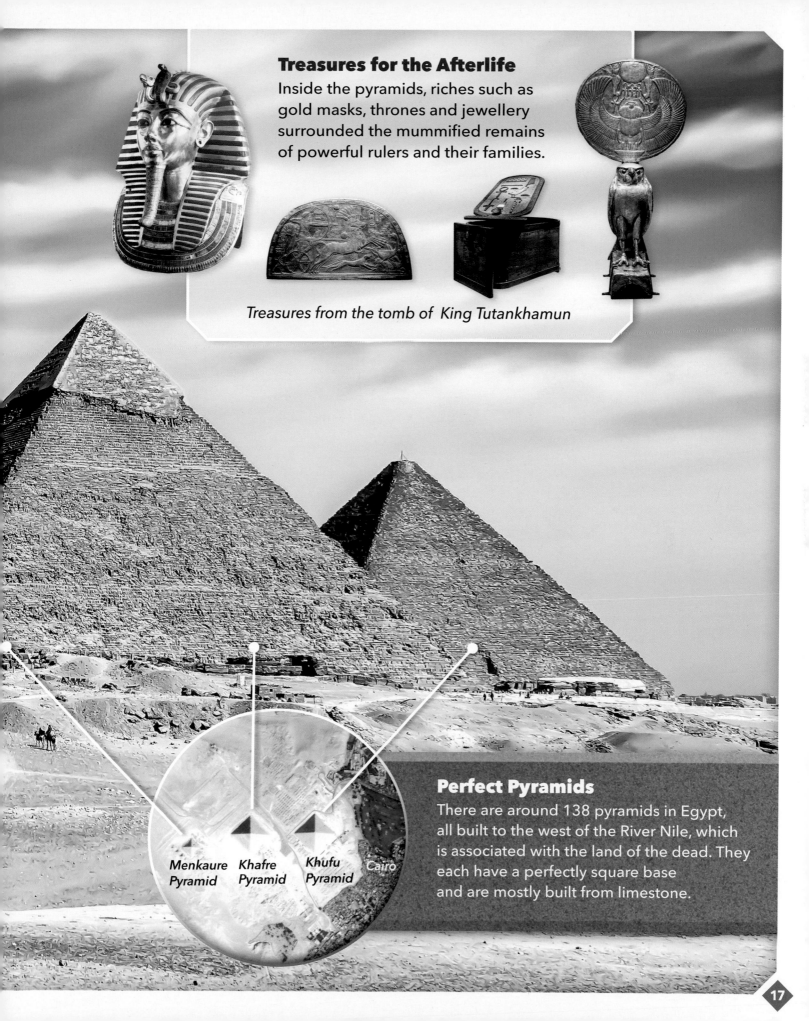

Treasures for the Afterlife

Inside the pyramids, riches such as gold masks, thrones and jewellery surrounded the mummified remains of powerful rulers and their families.

Treasures from the tomb of King Tutankhamun

Menkaure Pyramid   Khafre Pyramid   Khufu Pyramid   Cairo

Perfect Pyramids

There are around 138 pyramids in Egypt, all built to the west of the River Nile, which is associated with the land of the dead. They each have a perfectly square base and are mostly built from limestone.

The Great Pyramid of Khufu

The oldest and largest pyramid in Giza was built for Pharaoh Khufu around 4,500 years ago. This huge structure reaches 147 metres high at its tip and each side of its square base measures 109 metres in length. Its four corners point perfectly towards north, east, south and west.

The Tallest Structure on Earth

For thousands of years, The Great Pyramid of Khufu was the tallest structure on Earth. It covers an area similar in size to about nine modern football fields and is estimated to have used two million huge stone blocks weighing up to 2,200 kilograms each.

Sleds, Ramps, Ropes and Pulleys

Today, archaeologists are still working to understand just how the ancient Egyptians were able to build such mammoth structures. Many experts believe that the heavy stones were pulled into place using sleds, ramps and a rope and pulley system. In 2018, archaeologists discovered an ancient ramp system in a 4,500-year-old quarry, which supports this theory.

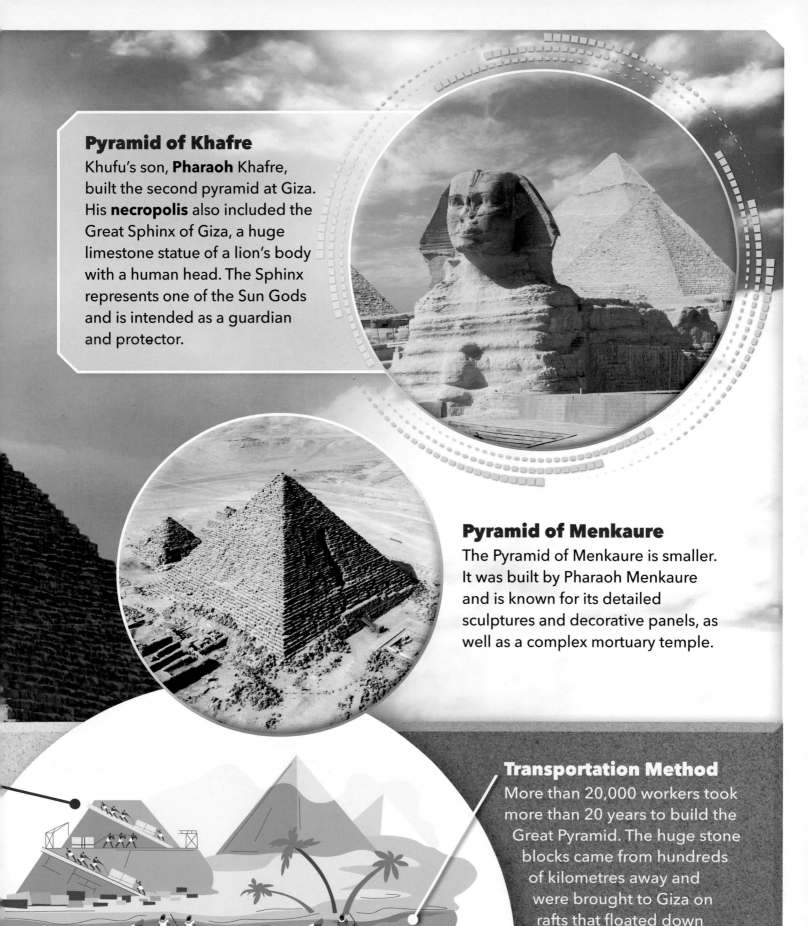

Pyramid of Khafre

Khufu's son, **Pharaoh** Khafre, built the second pyramid at Giza. His **necropolis** also included the Great Sphinx of Giza, a huge limestone statue of a lion's body with a human head. The Sphinx represents one of the Sun Gods and is intended as a guardian and protector.

Pyramid of Menkaure

The Pyramid of Menkaure is smaller. It was built by Pharaoh Menkaure and is known for its detailed sculptures and decorative panels, as well as a complex mortuary temple.

Transportation Method

More than 20,000 workers took more than 20 years to build the Great Pyramid. The huge stone blocks came from hundreds of kilometres away and were brought to Giza on rafts that floated down the River Nile.

THE GREAT WALL OF CHINA

Stretching over 20,000 kilometres, the Great Wall is China's most famous destination. The main wall is 6,300 kilometres in length, and some parts, being over 2,242 years old, have now fallen into ruin.

First Line of Defence

The Great Wall was the greatest military defence project in China's history. It included 25,000 watchtowers that had fire beacons to warn patrolling soldiers of an attack. There were barracks for soldiers on duty and towns were built along the wall, so that soldiers were always nearby if there was an attack. Wide moats were built outside the wall to make approach even more difficult.

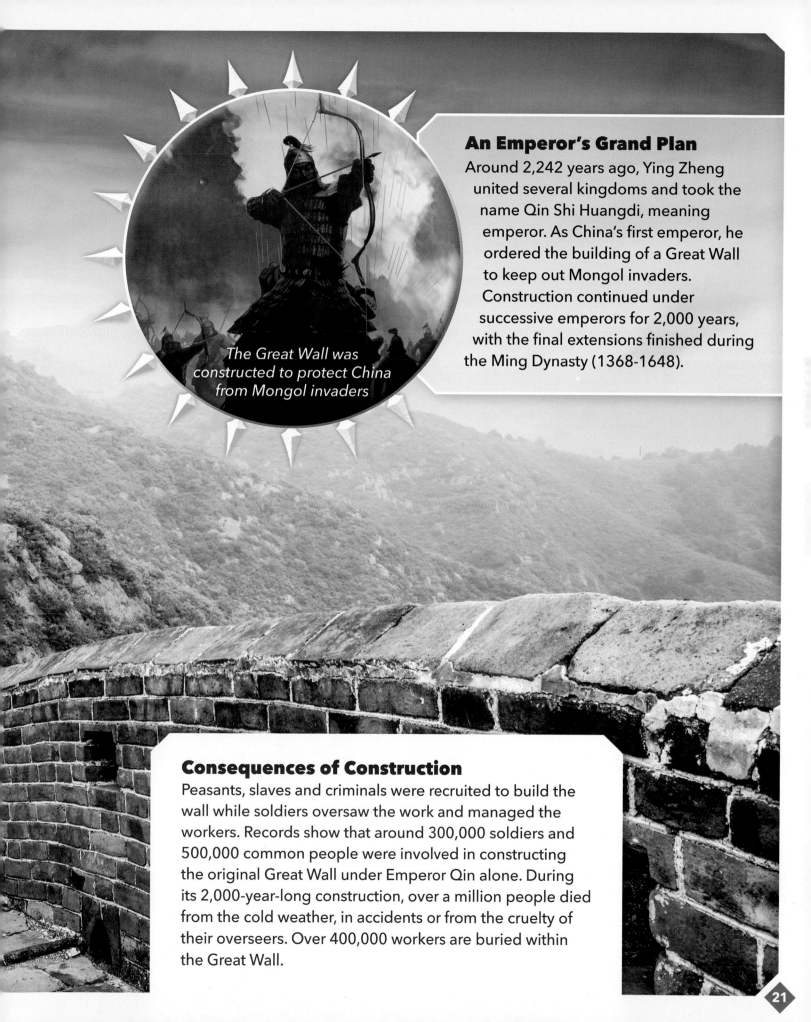

An Emperor's Grand Plan

Around 2,242 years ago, Ying Zheng united several kingdoms and took the name Qin Shi Huangdi, meaning emperor. As China's first emperor, he ordered the building of a Great Wall to keep out Mongol invaders. Construction continued under successive emperors for 2,000 years, with the final extensions finished during the Ming Dynasty (1368-1648).

The Great Wall was constructed to protect China from Mongol invaders

Consequences of Construction

Peasants, slaves and criminals were recruited to build the wall while soldiers oversaw the work and managed the workers. Records show that around 300,000 soldiers and 500,000 common people were involved in constructing the original Great Wall under Emperor Qin alone. During its 2,000-year-long construction, over a million people died from the cold weather, in accidents or from the cruelty of their overseers. Over 400,000 workers are buried within the Great Wall.

TERRACOTTA WARRIORS

Around 2,270 years ago, construction began on an army made out of terracotta rock. The purpose of this army was to protect the tomb of China's first emperor, Qin Shi Huang. Over 720,000 builders, stonemasons and artisans worked on the army for almost forty years. When construction was completed around 2,220 years ago, there were more than 8,000 stone warriors, 670 horses and 130 chariots.

The tomb remained untouched for 2,000 years until it was re-discovered in 1974 by local farmers. UNESCO inscribed the Terracotta Warriors as a Cultural World Heritage Site in 1987.

Personalised Structures

It is believed that the Terracotta Warriors were carved in the likeness of real people, as all the statues have different facial features, expressions, hairstyles and builds.

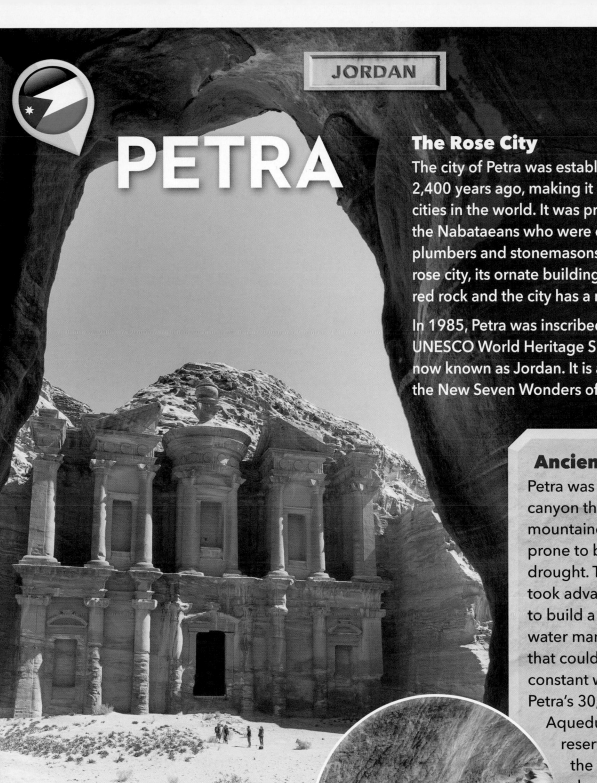

PETRA

The Rose City

The city of Petra was established around 2,400 years ago, making it one of the oldest cities in the world. It was primarily built by the Nabataeans who were excellent carvers, plumbers and stonemasons. Also known as the rose city, its ornate buildings are carved from red rock and the city has a rose-coloured hue.

In 1985, Petra was inscribed as a UNESCO World Heritage Site in what is now known as Jordan. It is also one of the New Seven Wonders of the World.

Ancient Technology

Petra was built in a desert canyon that bordered a mountainous area. It was prone to both flooding and drought. The Nabataeans took advantage of this to build a sophisticated water management system that could provide a constant water supply to Petra's 30,000 inhabitants. Aqueducts, cisterns and reservoirs controlled the floodwaters after heavy rain and stored the water to use during long periods of drought.

An aqueduct carved in rock at Al-Khazneh in Petra, Jordan

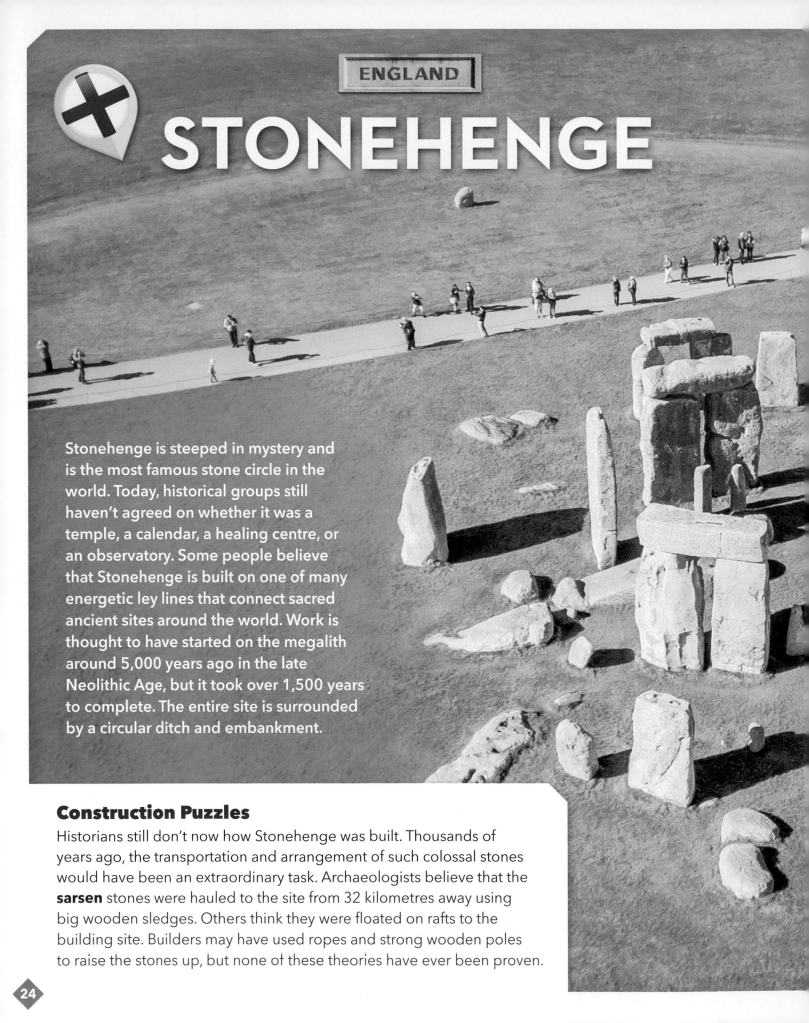

STONEHENGE

Stonehenge is steeped in mystery and is the most famous stone circle in the world. Today, historical groups still haven't agreed on whether it was a temple, a calendar, a healing centre, or an observatory. Some people believe that Stonehenge is built on one of many energetic ley lines that connect sacred ancient sites around the world. Work is thought to have started on the megalith around 5,000 years ago in the late Neolithic Age, but it took over 1,500 years to complete. The entire site is surrounded by a circular ditch and embankment.

Construction Puzzles

Historians still don't now how Stonehenge was built. Thousands of years ago, the transportation and arrangement of such colossal stones would have been an extraordinary task. Archaeologists believe that the **sarsen** stones were hauled to the site from 32 kilometres away using big wooden sledges. Others think they were floated on rafts to the building site. Builders may have used ropes and strong wooden poles to raise the stones up, but none of these theories have ever been proven.

Fun Facts about Stonehenge

- Stonehenge is one of over 1,300 stone circles found in the UK

- About one million people visit Stonehenge every year

- The smaller stones are called bluestones because they have a blue tinge when wet

- Some of the stones came from Wales and their transportation to the site remains a mystery

- The circle is built with mathematical precision, precisely matching the direction of the midsummer sunrise and midwinter sunset, and the movements of the moon

- There are 83 stones at Stonehenge of two different types of stone

- The larger stones are called sarsens which stand upto 9 metres tall and weigh around 22,500 kilograms each

- The largest of the stones weighs over 40,000 kilograms

THE PARTHENON

The most famous temple of the ancient world is nestled atop the **Acropolis**, a Greek word that means upper city or high hill. The Acropolis, or 'sacred rock' of Athens is an ancient citadel located on a rocky outcrop above the Greek capitol. Originally, the Acropolis was the stronghold of the early Athenian kings and became the city's religious centre.

The Acropolis is home to several ancient buildings of great architectural and historical significance. The most famous of these structures is the Parthenon.

Athene, Patron of Athens

Athene, also known as Athena, is an ancient Greek goddess associated with wisdom, handicraft and warfare. In Greek mythology, Athene was born from the head of her father, Zeus.

The Changing faces of the Parthenon

- In the year 435, Byzantine Emperor Theodosius closed all Pagan temples including the Parthenon

- In the late 6th century the Parthenon became a Christian Church

- In 1456 it was converted to a mosque

- In 1687 it was used as a gunpowder store

Flawless Foundations

This dazzling temple, with its white marble columns, was built to honour Athene, the city's patron goddess. Phidias designed the Parthenon, while **architects** Ictinos and Callicrates supervised construction.

The Parthenon has enormous limestone foundations. The base measures 69.49 metres by 30.78 metres. The structure stands at 13.71 metres tall and is made from Pentelic marble, mined from quarries in Pentelli, north of Athens. It was the first time the flawless Pentelic marble was ever used.

NEWGRANGE

An Ancient Irish Tomb

Newgrange is a 5,200-year-old passage tomb, located in the Republic of Ireland. Built by Stone Age farmers, the circular top is about the size of a modern-day football field. The mound is 85 metres in diameter and 13.5 metres high.

There are 97 large stones called kerbstones surrounding Newgrange. Some of these are engraved with megalithic art.

Kerbstones at Newgrange

Temple of Light

An entrance on the south-western side opens into a 19-metre long passage that leads into a chamber with three alcoves. The passage and chamber are aligned with the rising sun at the **winter solstice**. On roughly four days every year, the winter solstice sun pokes through the top of this Stone Age monument and onto the floor of the interior chamber, filling the ancient temple with light for about 17 minutes.

Ancient STRUCTURES

Around **30,000 years ago**, petroglyphs began being carved in the Burrup Peninsula

Around **9,000 years ago**, people began living in the area that was to become Petra

Around **7,000 years ago**, the arrangement of the Carnac Stones began

Around **5,600 years ago**, construction began on the Megalithic Temples of Malta

Around **12,000 years ago**, construction began on Göbekli Tepe

Around **9,000 years ago**, construction began on the Burrup Peninsula structures

Around **6,600 years ago**, construction began on the Budj Bim Eel Traps

Around **5,200 years ago**, construction began on Newgrange

TIMELINE

Around
5,000 years ago,
construction began
on Stonehenge

Around
2,540 years ago,
construction began
on Persepolis,
the Gate of Nations

Around
2,400 years ago,
construction began on
Petra city

Around
2,240 years ago,,
construction began on the
Great Wall of China

Around
4,500 years ago,
construction began on the
Great Pyramid of Khufu

Around
2,470 years ago,
construction began on
the Parthenon

Around
2,270 years ago,
construction began on the
Terracotta Warriors

Around
1,950 years ago,
construction began on
the Colosseum

Index

Glossary

architect ....person who designs a building

Acropolis..................ancient Greek fortified city located on a rocky outcrop or hill

amphitheatre ....open-air theatre with a circular or oval arena and tiered seating

archaeologist ....person who studies history through excavation sites and analysis of artefacts

necropolis................cemetery belonging to an ancient city

Pharaoh ....Egyptian king

pyramid....................tomb for an Egyptian king

sarsen ....large sandstone blocks found in England, used in constructing Stonehenge

winter solstice........time when the sun reaches its lowest midday point in the sky